KNOCK KNOCK JOKES

BIRD BRAINS

NICKY BIRD

FOLK LORE PUBLISHING

The Publisher: Folklore Publishing Ltd.
Website: www.folklorepublishing.com

Library and Archives Canada Cataloguing in Publication

Bird, Nicky, 1961–, author

   Knock knock jokes : bird brains / Nicky Bird.

ISBN 978-1-926677-96-5 (paperback)

   1. Knock-knock jokes. 2. Wit and humor, Juvenile. I. Title.

PN6231.K55B57   2016 jC818'.602   C2015-907833-4

Cover images: Front cover: Thinkstock: bandian1122; Cory Thoman; nazilart; Tigatelu. *Back cover:* Thinkstock: bandian1122; HitToon; musri; nazilart.

Background images: Thinkstock: B-A-C-O, 0–11, 20–21, 30–31, 40–41, 50–51, 60–61; sababaJJ, 6–7, 16–17, 26–27, 36–37, 46–47, 56–57; William Bacon, 4–5, 8–9, 14–15, 18–19, 24–25, 28–29, 34–35, 38–39, 44–45, 48–49, 54–55, 58–59;Yuriy Kozoriz, 2–3, 12–13, 22–23, 32–33, 42–43, 52–53, 62–63.

Image credits: Thinkstock: Arvila, 9, 13, 46; bandian 1122, 2, 3, 5, 9–11, 13, 14,16, 20–22, 25, 27, 29, 31, 34, 35, 37, 38, 40, 41, 44, 45, 47–50, 53–55, 59, 60, 62, 63, 54, 57; Christos Georghiou, 8, 18, 27, 39, 52, 58; Cory Thoman, 4, 8, 9, 12, 16, 17, 20, 23, 24, 26, 28, 33, 36, 38, 39, 45, 49, 50, 53, 54, 62; HitToon, 4, 5, 9, 10, 14, 15, 17–19, 21, 24, 25, 28, 36–38, 40, 46, 47, 56, 59; memoangeles, 6, 7, 13, 15, 30, 32, 33, 42, 43, 48, 51, 55,57, 61; musri, 6, 7, 11, 15, 19, 32, 33, 37, 40, 42, 43, 51, 56, 61; nazlisart, 2, 3, 17, 20, 21, 23, 29, 34, 35, 40, 41, 46, 53, 57, 60; nyamol, 6, 12, 14, 25, 32, 38, 42, 52, 56, 58; Onoontour, 4, 5, 19, 23, 26, 30, 36, 41, 52, 58; Tigatelu, 5–8, 10–15, 18, 24, 30, 32, 33, 37, 39, 42, 43, 49, 51–53, 57–59, 61, 62; Yael Weiss; 8, 16, 26, 28, 31, 39, 44, 48, 50, 55.

Produced with the assistance of the Government of Alberta, Alberta Media Fund.

We acknowledge the financial support of the Government of Canada through the Canada Book Fund (CBF) for our publishing activities.

 Canadian Patrimoine
Heritage   canadien

PC: 30